USES FOR MOOSES

AND OTHER SILLY OBSERVATIONS

Photographs by Paul Cyr

Down East Books

Published by Down East Books

An imprint of Globe Pequot

Distributed by NATIONAL BOOK NETWORK

Photos © 2017 by Paul Cyr

Text © by Rowman & Littlefield

Design by Diana Nuhn

British Library Cataloguing in Publication Information Available

Library of Congress Cataloging-in-Publication Data Available

ISBN 978-1-60893-639-7 (hardcover)

ISBN 978-1-60893-640-3 (electronic)

∞™The paper used in this publication meets the minimum requirements of American National Standard for Information Sciences—Permanence of Paper for Printed Library Materials, ANSI/NISO Z39.48-1992.

Printed in the United States of America

Swamp Thing

These backwoods triathlons are brutal. By the time I finish the running and swimming parts, I'm all done.

That age-old quandary: Why did the moose cross the road?

Crash test dummies.

Let's follow those hikers,
and when they're not looking
we'll steal their trail mix.

This is my best side, though really, my other side isn't too shabby, either.

Psst... hey, you... yeah, you... can I interest you in a Christmas tree?

Presidential candidate—
all wet and full of bull.

When you get in line
at the DMV.

Act natural, the humans are staring again.

El Toro Loco

Sorry bub, up here in moose country we have the right-of-way.

Swing your partner
round and round.

A creature only a mama
could love. Guess that
makes me the mama.

Dammit, why did giraffes get the long neck? What, I don't have anything to reach?

Times like this I wish I was
a bear so I could hole up
for the winter.

Seen only on the foggiest days, it's . . .
the Phantom Moose.

Some majestic, ain't he?

This highly tuned body is
the result of a strict
raw-paleo-vegan diet.

1 moose, 2 moose, 3 moose, 4;

5 moose, 6 moose, 7 moose, more;

8 moose, 9 ... aw, the heck with it.

How many moose do you see?

Up periscope.

Organic floss, because we moose are all about natural oral hygiene.

It's a bit early, and there's no mistletoe, but what the heck.

I don't know what these plants are, but that farmer sure gets mad when I step on them.

One more crack about hat racks and we'll show you what else they're good for.

"I GOTTA BE ME...
I GOTTA BE—"
"Oh, shut up, you'll wake the
whole north woods."

You don't think my nose
is too big, do you?

Rebel Moose Without a Cause

What are you looking at? The sign says "Moose Crossing" for a reason.

Next season's Patriots defensive line.

My Uber should be right along.

Antler wrestling—

no thumbs required.

Hood ornament.

I know they'll grow back in the spring, but losing them every fall just gives me the blahs.

The rare and mysterious
double-ender.

Antlers, yo.

Real moose or shadow puppet?

Demon Moose

There's no way we lose
Westminster this year.

Yeah, moose do it in the woods, too. A little privacy, please.

I'd like to have a word with this Bambi character about who's the real king of the forest.

You might think you're coming
this way, but you ain't.

Call SETI,
I'm picking up some mighty
strange signals.

Moose in sheep's clothing.

It's not a Dunkin' turbo shot,
but it sure is refreshing.

What kind of moosepower
do you get in that thing?

A couple more and we'll have enough for a baseball team. Now, who knows how to play?

Hide-and-seek is not
my favorite game.

The morning after
the bachelor party.

Mooz 'n the Hood,
aka The Squad

When you really want
to go swimming, but
the water is too cold.

Dude, don't look now, but I think she's checking you out.

I'm not really famoose,
but I oughta be.

Everything is bigger in
moose country. In golf
a par 40 is the norm.

Bullwinkle was an idiot.

Forget the all-seeing eye,
this nose knows.

Great, we're lost and
we're going to be late—
all because you're too stubborn
to ask for directions.

If you're looking for trouble,
I'll accommodate you.